The ODDBALL Book of ARMADILLOS

Elizabeth Shreeve

illustrated by
Isabella Grott

Norton Young Readers
An Imprint of W. W. Norton & Company
Independent Publishers Since 1923

For Mariella, Greg, and other scientists who uncover the wonders of life on Earth, present and past.
—E. S.

This book is dedicated to animals and to those who love and protect them. Without these creatures, this world wouldn't be so charming and fascinating.
—I. G.

Printed in China
First Edition

For information about permission to reproduce selections from this book, write to Permissions, W. W. Norton & Company, Inc., 500 Fifth Avenue, New York, NY 10110

For information about special discounts for bulk purchases, please contact W. W. Norton Special Sales at specialsales@wwnorton.com or 800-233-4830

Manufacturing by RRD Asia
Book design by Hana Anouk Nakamura
Production manager: Delaney Adams

ISBN 978-1-324-05218-0

W. W. Norton & Company, Inc., 500 Fifth Avenue, New York, N.Y. 10110
www.wwnorton.com

W. W. Norton & Company Ltd., 15 Carlisle Street, London W1D 3BS

1 2 3 4 5 6 7 8 9 0

ARMADILLOS

Are they giant roly-poly bugs?

Time-traveling dinosaurs?

Crazy mixed-up turtle-rabbits?

No! They're armadillos, the only mammals with bony outside coverings called *carapaces*. You may have seen these little critters snuffling through the woods around sunset. But did you know there are many different types of armadillos—and some of their prehistoric relatives grew as large as cars?

Well, pull on your boots.

It's time to track down some real, live . . .

. . . oddballs!

MEET THE ODDBALLS

With their tough, scaly coverings, armadillos seem to fit with the reptiles, alongside snakes, turtles, or crocodiles. *Surprise!* They are mammals, like us: warm-blooded animals that give birth to live young, nurse their babies with milk, and grow hair.

The name *armadillo* comes from a sixteenth-century Spanish word meaning "little armored one." But here's another surprise: some armadillo ancestors were enormous! Imagine a bunch of giant oddballs, trundling around with full suits of armor from head to tail. Wow!

Today, scientists count twenty-three living species of armadillos—smaller but no less amazing than their prehistoric relatives. Why did they change over time? Where are they headed? To find out, we'll travel through time to compare modern armadillos with their relatives from long ago.

Three-banded armadillo

Screaming hairy armadillo

Nine-banded armadillo

Pink fairy armadillo

Yup! It's an Armadillo!

Armadillos have tough, flexible carapaces and sharp claws for digging. Some species are named for the number of flexible bands on their armor that allow them to twist and bend. Read on to discover which one can roll up in a ball!

TRAVELiNG NORTH

Across the southern United States, nine-banded armadillos are traveling north. In the dark of night, they waddle through swamps and along streams. They rustle through leaves, slurping up insects with long, sticky tongues before burrowing underground to sleep.

These days, most armadillos live in South America. But around 1849, some nine-banded armadillos crossed the Rio Grande into Texas and began spreading into Louisiana, Mississippi, and Oklahoma. Florida's thriving population started when a few animals escaped a private zoo in 1924. Ten years later, more broke loose from a circus! Nine-banded armadillos now find happy homes in parts of Colorado, Nebraska, Illinois, and other states. One was found all the way up in South Dakota, possibly after hitchhiking on a hay truck.

So far, winters are too harsh for nine-banded armadillos to move farther north. But as the climate warms, how far will they spread?

Let's find some clues, starting long ago . . .

RANGE: Central United States through Mexico, Central America, and northern and central South America; Caribbean islands of Grenada and Trinidad and Tobago
MAXIMUM SIZE: 22 inches long (plus 18-inch tail); 13 pounds
STATUS: Least Concern

Nine-Banded Armadillo (*Dasypus novemcinctus*)

Nine-banded armadillos inhabit the largest territory of all armadillos, from South America through Central America, Mexico, and south-central United States. A number of adaptations help them thrive. They sleep in their burrows during the day and forage under cover of darkness. They prefer wet, warm forested areas but don't mind living near people. And mothers give birth to four genetically identical babies, a reproductive strategy that appears to increase populations quickly.

These resilient animals, also known as common long-nosed armadillos, gobble up all kinds of insects, including fire ants. They also eat scarab beetles, insects that can devastate crops. But, despite rumors, they do not raid chicken coops for eggs or dig up dead bodies! Nine-banded armadillos have occasionally been known to carry leprosy, a disease that also affects humans, so it's best to leave them alone.

Beautiful Armadillo (*Dasypus bellus*)

Like the nine-banded armadillo, the beautiful armadillo moved into North America seeking warm, wet habitats with plenty of insects to eat. One fossil discovery included an adult with four babies, suggesting that beautiful armadillos produced quadruplets, too.

But scientists point to differences. Fossils of beautiful armadillos are often found in caves rather than in burrows. They were bigger, about twice the size of the nine-banded armadillo, which may have helped them to tolerate colder temperatures. They might even have grown warm coats like the hairy armadillos that inhabit South America today.

PREHISTORIC RAMBLERS

Armadillos originated in South America around 60 million years ago. They reached North America in prehistoric times, too.

Some were tank-like giants. Others were medium-sized plant-eaters that grazed on the coarse grasses of their new home. These South American natives rambled through Central America, parts of Mexico, and the southeastern United States.

The beautiful armadillo traveled farthest of all. This animal looked like today's nine-banded armadillos but grew to over twice their size. It occupied a similar range, though it ambled farther northward into places that today's armadillos find too chilly for comfort. At least so far!

RANGE: Central South America to south-central North America
MAXIMUM SIZE: 48 inches long; 40 pounds
TIME PERIOD: 1.8 million years ago to 11,000 years ago
NAME MEANS: "Pretty Hairy-Foot"

Early Journeys

Ever notice how South America's eastern coastline fits like a puzzle piece into the western edge of Africa? That's because the two continents were once part of a supercontinent called Pangea. About 200 million years ago, Pangea began to break apart due to forces deep within the earth. By around 140 million years ago, South America had split from Africa to become an island continent. Its animal passengers, including the distant ancestors of armadillos, evolved into unique creatures found only in the New World.

Then around 3 million years ago, a land bridge finished forming between North and South America. This triggered an event known as the Great American Biotic Interchange, or GABI. Carnivores like cougars, wolves, and bears moved southward, as did hoofed animals like tapirs, deer, and horses. Armadillos moved northward alongside ground sloths and other South American immigrants. Some grew to enormous sizes and became part of the *Ice Age megafauna*, which included giant ground sloths, woolly mammoths, dire wolves, and saber-toothed cats. These super-sized animals disappeared around 10,000 years ago, possibly due to a combination of impacts including a warming climate and hunting and habitat modification by humans.

Today only three South American natives inhabit North America: armadillos, porcupines, and opossums.

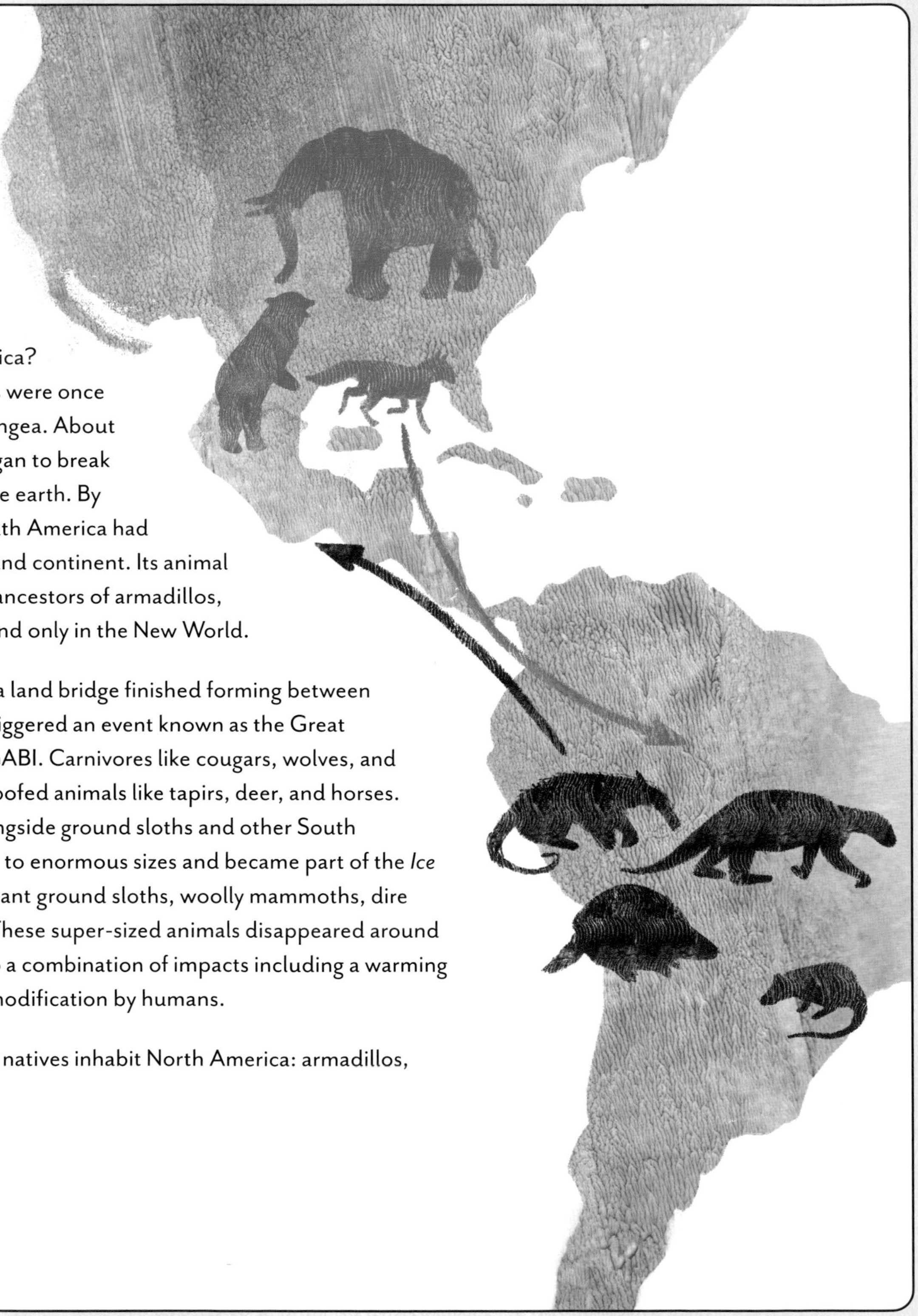

Official State Mammals of Texas

In 1995, Texas schoolchildren held a mock election to pick an official state mammal. It was a perfect tie! Half of the kids voted for the longhorn, a type of cattle, while the other half championed the armadillo.

Texas politicians found a compromise. They designated the longhorn as the state's official large mammal, while the nine-banded armadillo became the official small mammal. The legislation praised armadillos as hardy, pioneering creatures with "attributes that distinguish a true Texan, such as a deep respect and need for the land, the ability to change and adapt, and a fierce undying love for freedom."

LiFE ON THE HALF-SHELL

Quick! Think of an animal with a hard, outer shell.

Does a lobster come to mind? A turtle?

An armored dinosaur?

Don't forget the armadillo! Its tough carapace protects it from predators and thorny underbrush. A small shield covers the animal's head, like a miniature helmet. Two other parts cover the body—one for the front and one for the hindquarters, with flexible bands in between. Some types of armadillos even have rings of bones around their tails.

Over time, this basic design has given rise to a range of armadillos of many sizes and shapes. On the small end, a pink fairy armadillo could fit in the palm of your hand. It looks like a piece of shrimp sushi!

But long ago . . .

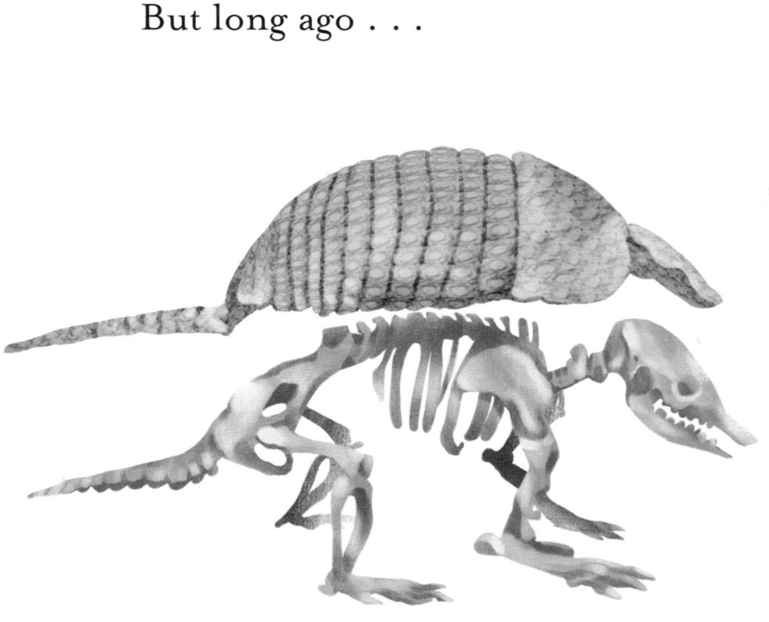

The carapace fits like a suit of armor.

Pink Fairy Armadillo (*Chlamyphorus truncatus*)

The smallest armadillo is also one of the most difficult to find. This elusive, nocturnal creature lives almost entirely underground. It can bury itself in seconds, using oversized claws and a specialized rear plate to dig a tunnel, backfilling as it goes. Its body is covered by white silky hair, and its rosy color comes from blood flow visible through a delicate carapace—features that help it adjust to changing temperatures in its desert home.

In parts of its range, the pink fairy armadillo has a reputation as a signal of bad fortune. Totally undeserved! In other regions, however, this remarkable animal is revered as a deity that needs to be protected.

RANGE: Portions of Central Argentina
MAXIMUM SIZE: 6 inches long; 4 ounces
STATUS: Data Deficient (insufficient information available)

Doedicurus

Doedicurus was one of the largest glyptodonts. With its massive shell and heavy tail club, it resembles an armored dinosaur like the ankylosaur or stegosaur—animals that had lived tens of millions of years earlier. The size and body shapes of this giant animal show how mammals took over many of the ecological roles of dinosaurs after the Mesozoic Era, known as the Age of Reptiles, came to an end.

Amazingly, recent DNA studies suggest that *Doedicurus* may be most closely related to its smallest living relative: the pink fairy armadillo.

RANGE: Cool, wet parts of South America, especially the grassy plains (Pampas) of Argentina and Uruguay
MAXIMUM SIZE: 13 feet long; over 2,400 pounds
TIME PERIOD: 2 million years ago to 10,000 years ago
NAME MEANS: "Pestle Tail"

BUILT LIKE A TANK

Some prehistoric armadillos were huge!

Glyptodonts were the largest, reaching the size of small cars and weighing up to two tons. That's as heavy as 16,000 pink fairy armadillos!

Unlike today's armadillos, glyptodonts clomped around under a solid dome of armor, like a tortoise's shell. These giants emerged in South America over 35 million years ago, growing larger over time. They spread to southern regions of North America after the two continents connected, leaving behind fossils from what is now Arizona eastward through the Carolinas.

One glyptodont, *Doedicurus*, had a spiked tail club that weighed over 100 pounds (that's 400 pink fairy armadillos, by the way).

The Stony Remains of Giants

In 1832, a young man named Charles Darwin collected fossils on a windy beach in Argentina. As naturalist aboard His Majesty's Ship *Beagle*, Darwin was pondering how life-forms change over time. How, he wondered, were the stony remains of giants that he found related to the live animals he observed—and sometimes ate for dinner? Darwin quite enjoyed a meal of armadillo, which, he wrote, "when fat & roasted is most excellent eating."

After returning to England, Darwin wrote a book called *On the Origin of Species* that laid out the principles of evolution, establishing the basis for modern life sciences. In an autobiography at the end of his life, Darwin mentions what inspired his vision—the "great fossil animals covered with armour like that of the existing armadillos."

Darwin noticed similarities between glypodont fossils and living armadillos.

Computer Scans and DNA

How do we know how prehistoric animals are related to modern ones?

Scientists start with fossilized bones, which show how prehistoric creatures looked and moved. They link fossils to time periods to trace how features like hip joints or skulls were passed down over time. At the Florida Museum of Natural History, researchers use computed tomography (CT) scanning of fossilized skulls to understand the brains of ancient armadillos and sloths. Molecular data, such as ancient DNA, can reveal even more. For example, scientists debated whether nine-banded armadillos are simply a smaller variation of beautiful armadillos—until DNA from fossils revealed that they are separate species.

Studying the living animals poses different challenges. It's hard to observe armadillos because they hide underground. Scientists Jim Loughry and Colleen McDonough report peering into a burrow—and coming face to face with a rattlesnake! Others have tried tickling an animal's belly to loosen its grip on a burrow.

Armadillos are also nocturnal, which means searching for them in the dark. One expert, Mariella Superina, has been studying pink fairy armadillos for almost 20 years and has never found a single one in its natural habitat. But she hasn't given up!

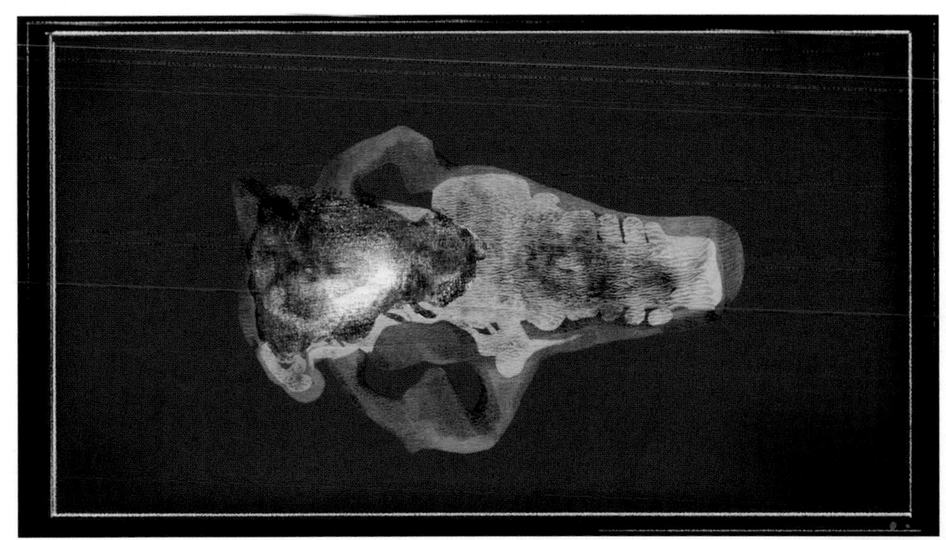

Computerized scan of a fossilized skull.

TOUGH DEFENDERS

They leap! They scream! They vanish underground!

Armadillos are tough. When their carapaces won't protect them, they use other defenses. A nine-banded armadillo jumps several feet into the air, startling a predator. It kicks and scratches with its long, razor-sharp claws, too, and can even flip itself over to land on and squash a snake. Screaming hairy armadillos make bloodcurdling squeals to avoid becoming a meal.

But armadillos have sometimes been hunters rather than prey.

Long ago . . .

Screaming Hairy Armadillo (*Chaetophractus vellerosus*)

It might look like a scrap of coconut shell with legs. But listen up!

When it's distressed, the screaming hairy armadillo pelts out earsplitting cries, sobs, gasps, and grunts. Wow! These little animals are also known for their thicker hair and adorable, extra-long ears. They inhabit dry, desert areas and can survive for long periods without water.

RANGE: Parts of Argentina, Bolivia, Paraguay, and Chile
MAXIMUM SIZE: 11 inches long (plus 4-inch tail); 2 pounds
STATUS: Least Concern; isolated populations are threatened

Macroeuphractus

For millions of years, the *Macroeuphractus* armadillos were "hyper-carnivores" in their ecosystems, meaning that over 70 percent of their diet was meat. Equipped with impressive rows of sharply pointed teeth and strong jaw-closing muscles, they probably hunted and scavenged for food. *Macroeuphractus* shared the role of predator alongside giant opossums and enormous terror birds, prior to the arrival of North American carnivores like jaguars and saber-toothed cats.

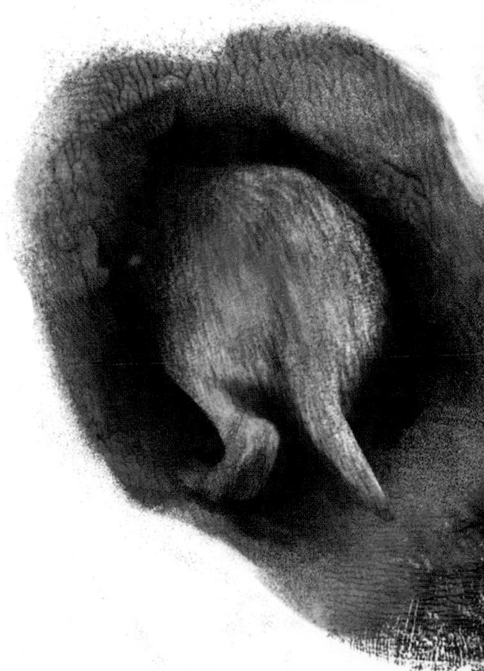

RANGE: Fossils discovered in central Argentina and Bolivia
MAXIMUM SIZE: 3 feet long; 200 pounds
TIME PERIOD: 9 million years ago to 3 million years ago
NAME MEANS: "Large Well-Protected"

FiERCE PREDATORS

Yikes! Look at those teeth!

Most prehistoric armadillos were herbivores, or plant-eaters. Today's armadillos are omnivores that eat insects and plants. But an ancestor of hairy armadillos, called *Macroeuphractus*, was a flesh-eating predator with sharp teeth and powerful jaws. It was likely a good runner, too, and able to dig animals out of their underground hiding places, as badgers do today. This tough, leopard-sized animal competed with fierce hunters of its time like the enormous, flightless terror birds.

Hmmm . . . who would you choose to win that battle?

Bone-Skin

An armadillo's carapace consists of small bony plates inside the skin called *osteoderms*, meaning "bone-skin." Each osteoderm is covered by keratin, the same material as our fingernails. In some cases, such as with giant armadillos, scientists can identify an individual animal through the unique pattern of its osteoderms, like a person's fingerprint.

Long ago, some types of now-extinct giant ground sloths also had pebble-like osteoderms embedded in their skin. But armadillos are the only living mammals with protective coverings made of osteoderms.

Wait—don't pangolins have hard outside coverings, too? *Yes!* Pangolins and armadillos were once thought to be related. New evidence, however, confirms that they developed similar traits but descended from different ancestors. In science, this is called *convergent evolution*. A closer look shows that pangolins grow overlapping scales made of keratin but lack the bony osteoderms of armadillos. Around 35 million years ago, pangolins inhabited Montana and other parts of North America. Today they live only in Africa and Asia.

Osteoderms of glypodonts, armadillos, and pampatheres

Pangolin

The Story of Teeth

How do scientists determine the diets of ancient animals? By their teeth, of course!

The size, shape, and quantity of teeth give clues to a creature's lifestyle, millions of years after it munched on its last meal. The large, pointed front teeth of *Macroeuphractus* reveal its role as a carnivore. The deeply grooved teeth of glyptodonts tell us that these giants grazed on grass. Today, nine-banded armadillos grow about 30 cone-shaped "peg" teeth in their mouths—perfect for a diet of insects and plants.

And, as we'll see, one other modern armadillo grows many, many more teeth.

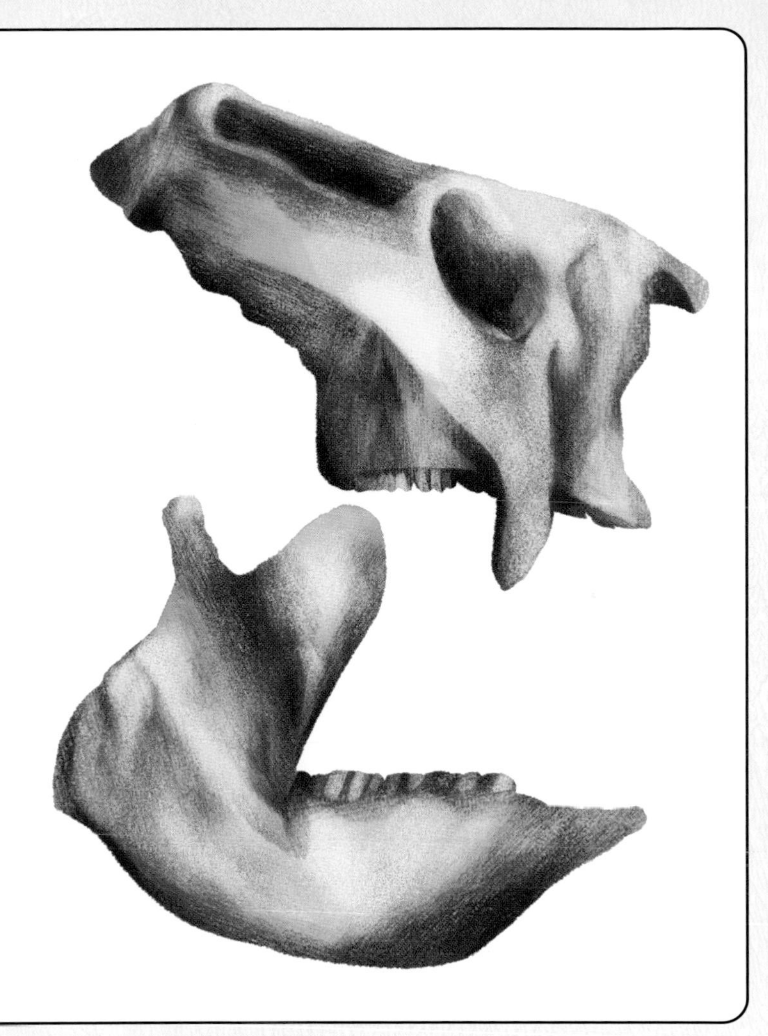

MASTER DiGGERS

Armadillos love to dig.

Special joints in their lower backs, combined with sharp claws, enable them to carve safe burrows for resting and hiding. They can tolerate the humid, low-oxygen conditions of underground life, too.

No armadillo is better equipped for digging than the giant armadillo. It has the largest claws of any living mammal—8 inches long! This species grows up to 100 teeth, too, and has a big appetite for insects. *Sniff-sniff.* A giant armadillo stands on its back legs next to a termite mound. *Rip-rip!* It tears into the mound and captures dinner with its long, sticky tongue. *Slurp!* It gobbles up many thousands of ants or termites in a single night.

But digging superpowers are nothing new in the armadillo family.

Long ago . . .

Giant Armadillo (*Priodontes maximus*)

This largest of today's armadillos has thick, powerful claws on its forefeet, causing it to walk on tiptoe like a ballet dancer. Its curved, extra-long middle claw works like a pickax to tear open insect nests. After completely demolishing the nest, giant armadillos will bury themselves in the remains and take a long snooze before setting off again.

Giant armadillos are rare, secretive animals. Using motion-sensing cameras, researchers in the vast Pantanal wetland of Brazil have observed them digging a new shelter every other night. Their abandoned burrows provide refuge for many other animals, including anteaters, lizards, small deer, and ocelots (pictured here). Their digging activities also help to turn the soil, uprooting more food and encouraging healthy plant growth. Giant armadillos are ecosystem engineers!

RANGE: Northern and central South America
MAXIMUM SIZE: 40 inches long (plus 19-inch tail); 90 pounds
STATUS: Vulnerable; threatened by hunting and habitat loss

Horned Armadillo (*Peltephilus*)

Check out this face! The horn-like spikes of *Peltephilus*, a dog-sized cousin of armadillos, are formed from the armor covering its head. Only one other burrow-dwelling mammal had horns on its face: the extinct horned gophers of North America.

Gophers and armadillos with horns? Why? Did horns help with digging, hunting, . . . or maybe defense against predators? No one knows for sure. *Peltephilus* was unique in other ways, too. Unlike most armadillos, its snout was wide and short. And its carapace consisted of a loose fabric of square-shaped osteoderms, like a built-in set of chain mail armor.

ANCIENT CLAWS

Armadillo ancestors were also strong diggers. Some ancient "paleoburrows" have claw marks on the walls and roofs. Imagine an enormous armadillo, long ago, digging a deep, safe den while a saber-toothed cat prowled nearby . . .

Quick, dig, hide!

Those strong claws had other uses, too. Armadillo ancestors dug up roots and small animals to eat, just as armadillos dig for food today. But some armadillo ancestors, like glyptodonts, may have been too big to burrow. They depended on their thick armor to protect them from predators. And those large bodies had other advantages—especially when the weather turned cold.

RANGE: South America; fossils found in Argentina, Bolivia, and Chile
MAXIMUM SIZE: 40 inches (including tail); 24 pounds
TIME PERIOD: 25 million years ago to 10 million years ago
NAME MEANS: "Small Shield-Loving"

Living Underground

Would you like to live in a burrow?

Warning: There's not much air down there. Soon you'll get dizzy and faint. Dirt will fall into your eyes even though they're closed because, well, it's pitch dark. And don't wander off because you might not find your way back.

Armadillos, on the other hand, have adapted to life underground. While their eyesight is poor—nine-banded armadillos sometimes run straight into trees when startled—their sense of smell is strong. Wiry hairs along their sides and bellies help them feel their way, like a cat's whiskers. They can even tolerate bad air quality. Small structures in their nostrils act like filters, closing together to block soil particles from entering. They are underground experts!

Keeping Babies Safe

Deep in a burrow, armadillo babies are born helpless, with soft, leathery carapaces. Moms keep them safe, even blocking the entrance with plants or soil when heading off to find food.

Family life varies between different species. Giant armadillo mothers give birth to a single baby every other year, and they spend at least a full year together as the youngster learns to explore and forage. The four identical quadruplets of nine-banded armadillos forage together for a summer, but the littermates soon split apart and lead solitary lives as adults.

WHEN THE TEMPERATURE DROPS . . .

Brrrrr! Armadillos do not like the cold. Their body temperatures run low. And without much fur or fat as insulation, they lose heat quickly through their carapaces and run the risk of freezing in their burrows.

Some armadillos have adapted by growing longer hair. One armadillo goes into a long hibernation when the weather turns chilly. Most types of armadillos, however, solve the problem by sticking to warmer areas. For today's armadillos, this limits how far they are likely to travel.

But long ago . . .

Pichi (*Zaedyus pichiy*)

Who's the coolest armadillo? The pichi!

During winter, this little creature burrows down to hibernate until conditions warm up. Its body temperature drops as low as 58 degrees Fahrenheit. (Compare that to a person's average temperature of around 98 degrees Fahrenheit.) Pichis can also enter brief hibernations, or *torpors*, to save energy when food or water is scarce. These adaptations enable them to inhabit colder areas, such as the Patagonia region at the southern tip of South America.

Pichis are also called dwarf armadillos. The name *pichi* means "little one" in the native language of the Mapuche, indigenous inhabitants of southern Chile and Argentina.

RANGE: Southern regions of Argentina and Chile
MAXIMUM SIZE: 12 inches long (plus 5-inch tail); 3 pounds
CONSERVATION STATUS: Near Threatened; impacted by hunting

Holmesina septentrionalis

Holmesina was one of the pampatheres that roamed farther north than most. A few million years ago, they traveled north during the Great American Biotic Interchange. The fossils of one species, *Holmesina septentrionalis*, have been found as far north as Kanopolis, Kansas, and across Texas, Oklahoma, Florida, and Mexico.

The *pampathere* got its name from the South American grassy plains known as Pampas, where they grazed on coarse vegetation. Their lineage branched off early in the armadillo family history. Yet they looked like large versions of modern armadillos, with three flexible bands in the carapace. The armadillo's unique armor has truly stood the test of time!

Holmesina septentrionalis
ranged into North America.

RANGE: Central South America and south-central North America
MAXIMUM SIZE: 72 inches long; 500 pounds
TIME PERIOD: 4.9 million years ago to 12,000 years ago
NAME MEANS: *Pampathere* means "Pampas Beast"

IT PAYS TO BE BIG

Some of the big prehistoric armadillos ranged into colder climes. Large bodies have less surface area relative to weight, so they lose less heat. That's why animals near the North and South Poles tend to be more massive, like polar bears of today and the woolly mammoths of long ago.

Millions of years ago, enormous glyptodonts reached southern portions of Argentina. Armadillo cousins known as *pampatheres* also tolerated cooler conditions. They trundled around many parts of South America and across the land bridge to North America. But even the largest members of the family avoided ice and snow. When it comes to weather, armadillos prefer to stay cozy and warm.

Walking Under Water

Cold weather will stop an armadillo, but they don't mind a swim.

Armadillos can hold their breath for six minutes at a time. By inflating their stomachs and floating—or by simply walking along the bottom—many types of armadillos can cross waterways with ease. Giant armadillos use rivers to travel. Nine-banded armadillos even crossed the mighty Rio Grande from Mexico into the United States.

Slowly but surely, armadillos move across the landscape of the Americas.

What happens when they meet people?

Armadillo Art

Thousands of years ago, an artist painted armadillos, red deer, jaguars, tapirs, and other animals on a cave wall. Set high in the steep, rocky cliffs of northeastern Brazil, those images of the ancient forest are among the earliest rock art in the Americas.

Armadillos have inspired jewelry, pottery, paintings, and sculpture by generations of indigenous peoples from Argentina to Mexico. Recently, a three-banded armadillo served as the official mascot for the 2014 soccer World Cup in Brazil. The carapaces of hairy armadillos are sometimes used for a guitar-like instrument called *charango*, a practice that is now illegal in most places due to overhunting.

Hey, Get Off My Lawn!

Today, in the United States, nine-banded armadillos are sometimes considered nuisances that dig up lawns and gardens. They are often spotted as roadkill on country roads. This has earned them an unfortunate nickname: "Texas speedbumps."

At the same time, nine-banded armadillos help to control insects that can damage crops. Medical scientists use them for researching a disease called leprosy, while bioengineers draw inspiration from their carapaces to design protective shields for people. And like giant armadillos, the burrows of nine-banded armadillos provide shelter for many species of birds, snakes, crabs, rodents, and other wildlife. Some experts believe they are filling the role of eco-engineer left by a native species, the gopher tortoise, whose numbers are in decline.

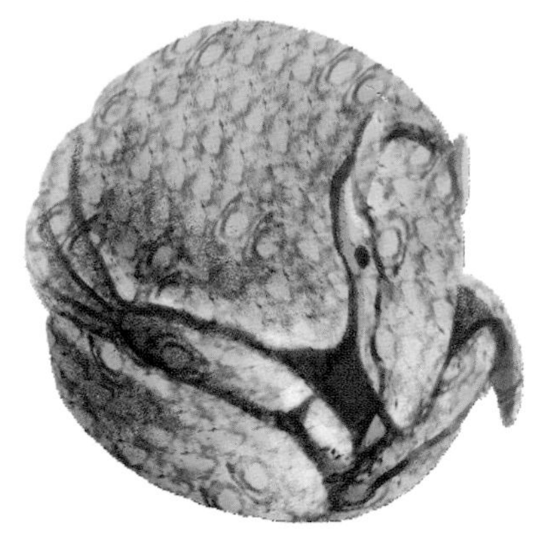

TOTAL ODDBALLS

So far, we've seen that armadillos grow armor like turtles. They speed-dig like moles, walk underwater like crabs, flip over onto snakes, and snuffle through the underbrush for insects like little bulldozers. Some grow long hair. Others hibernate like bears. They adapt to life in rainforests and deserts. In the past, they've grown to enormous sizes, wandered between continents, and carved out lives as gentle grazers and fierce, meat-hungry carnivores.

Okay, but you're probably wondering . . . can't they roll into balls?

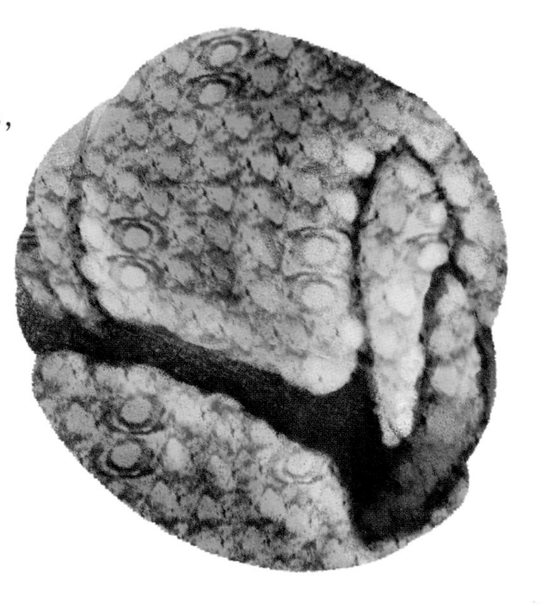

Yes! Three-banded armadillos defend themselves by curling into spheres about the size of a cantaloupe melon. One minute that little creature is waddling along like a wind-up toy and the next moment—*presto!* It's a total oddball.

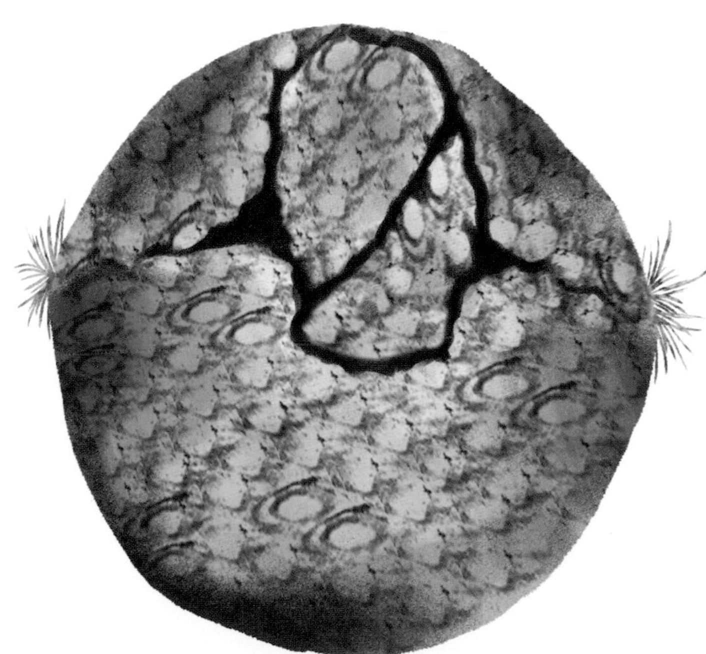

Three-Banded Armadillo (*Tolypeutes*)

How does a four-legged animal roll into a ball?

Three-banded armadillos perform this trick with the help of their unique carapaces, which are loose and unattached on the sides. When frightened, the animals react instantly. *Hop!* They curl inside their armor. *Tuck!* The triangular tail and head shield fit together like puzzle pieces. Sometimes they leave a small opening—just enough to close on a predator's hand or paw. *Snap!* All of the armadillo's body parts are protected, with no exposed flesh for a predator to hurt.

Compared to other armadillos, the three-banded are less likely to dig burrows. They often rest in shallow holes or nests, relying on their transformer-like skills for defense.

RANGE: Parts of Argentina, Bolivia, Brazil, and Paraguay
MAXIMUM SIZE: 12 inches long (plus 2.5-inch tail); 3 pounds
STATUS: Near Threatened (Southern three-banded) or Vulnerable (Brazilian three-banded); both species are impacted by hunting and habitat loss

ON THE MOVE

Life on Earth is constantly changing.

So what does the future hold for armadillos? Could there someday be an enormous, hairy, meat-eating, armor-protected armadillo that digs caves, grows horns, crosses wide rivers, and screams? Could a creature like that take over . . . everywhere?

Not likely. Many armadillos in South America, such as the pichi and giant armadillos, need our help to protect them and their habitats. But as the climate warms, nine-banded armadillos will continue to expand their range. With few natural predators to stop them, they'll reclaim territories where prehistoric armadillos once lived.

Will they cross mountains and deserts to California and on to Seattle? Could they trundle as far as Wyoming, New Hampshire, or even across the border to Canada?

Time will tell, but one thing's for sure: in North America, the hardy and pioneering nine-banded armadillo, official state small mammal of Texas, . . .

. . . is on the move!

TIMELINE OF ARMADILLO HISTORY

mya = million years ago
ya = years ago

Today: Twenty-three species of armadillos live in the Americas, primarily South America. Only one, the nine-banded, inhabits parts of North America.

1924: Nine-banded armadillos escape from a zoo in Florida; more escape from a circus in 1936

1849: Nine-banded armadillos first seen in Texas after crossing the Rio Grande

1839: Sir Richard Owen, famous British paleontologist, describes and classifies *Glyptodon*

1832: Charles Darwin finds glyptodont and giant ground sloth fossils in South America; these inspire his early thoughts on evolution

1551: First armadillo illustrated and described by Conrad Gessner, Swiss naturalist, in *Historia animalium* (History of the Animals)

10,000 ya: Glyptodonts, pampatheres, and other Ice Age species are extinct

2 mya to 12,000 ya: Beautiful armadillo (*Dasypus bellus*) evolves in South America and migrates into south-central parts of North America

3 mya: Isthmus of Panama land bridge connects North and South America. More glyptodonts, pampatheres, and others migrate northward as part of the Great American Biotic Interchange.

4 mya: *Holmesina* emerges in South America; later adapts and evolves in North America

9 to 3 mya: *Macroeuphractus* inhabits parts of South America; some glyptodonts and pampatheres find their way to Mexico

25 mya to 10 mya: *Peltephilus*, the horned armadillo, inhabits parts of South America

34 mya: Glyptodonts evolve in South America

45 to 3 mya: Armadillos diversify into new groups and species in South America

45 mya: *Dasypus* group of armadillos (ancestors of nine-banded) splits from other armadillos

53 mya: Date of earliest armadillo osteoderm fossils, found in southeastern Brazil

60 to 66 mya: Xenarthrans (armadillos, sloths, and anteaters) are emerging in South America. The Pilosa (sloths and anteaters) split from the Cingulata (armadillos).

66 mya: Dinosaur extinction; Age of Mammals begins

200 mya to 140 mya: Supercontinent of Pangea breaks apart; South America separates from Africa to become an isolated island continent

AUTHOR'S NOTE

I am profoundly grateful to the experts who guided my way through the enchanting world of armadillos. In particular, Dr. Mariella Superina of IUCN/SSC Anteater, Sloth, and Armadillo Specialist Group shared her knowledge and enthusiasm for modern species, while Dr. Greg McDonald of the US Bureau of Land Management (retired) contributed his remarkable understanding of prehistoric life.

Thanks also to Rachel Narducci at the Florida Museum, Dr. William J. (Jim) Loughry of Valdosta State University, and Dr. Richard Fariña of the Universidad de la República de Uruguay for reviewing drafts of the book. A special thanks to Dr. Loughry and Dr. Colleen McDonough for their generous hospitality. The work of these and other scientists builds our understanding and supports vital efforts for wildlife conservation.

Much appreciation to my agent, Ammi-Joan Paquette, and editor, Simon Boughton, for undertaking a book about oddballs. Huge thanks to Isabella Grott for beautiful artwork and to Hana Anouk Nakamura and others at Norton Young Readers for creative design and production. As always, I am grateful to family and writing comrades for supporting an author's obsession with some of nature's most curious creatures.

LEARN MORE

Mega Meltdown: The Weird and Wonderful Animals of the Ice Age, by Jack Tite. Blueprint Editions, 2018.

The Screaming Hairy Armadillo and 76 Other Animals with Weird, Wild Names, by Matthew Murrie and Steve Murrie. Workman Publishing Company, 2020.

"Armadillos: Nature's Armoured Miracles," *Wild America*, April 2021. Video on Real Wild YouTube Channel.

"Evolution of Armadillos," Moth Light Media, January 2020. Video on YouTube.

"Hotel Armadillo," PBS *Nature*, season 35, episode 14 (April 2017). Documentary at PBS.org.

Armadillo Online!: www.armadillo-online.org

IUCN/SSC Anteater, Sloth, and Armadillo Specialist Group: www.xenarthrans.org

American Museum of Natural History: www.amnh.org

Florida Museum: www.floridamuseum.ufl.edu

La Brea Tar Pits & Museum: www.tarpits.org

For Older Readers

Horned Armadillos and Rafting Monkeys: The Fascinating Fossil Mammals of South America, by Darin A. Croft. Indiana University Press, 2016.

Megafauna: Giant Beasts of Pleistocene South America, by Richard A. Fariña. Indiana University Press, 2013.

The Nine-Banded Armadillo: A Natural History, by W. J. Loughry and Colleen M. McDonough. University of Oklahoma Press, 2013.

For more learning, teaching, and conservation resources, please visit **www.elizabethshreeve.com**.